Unicorns in Underwear

An Awesome
Alphabet Book

By

Krishna and
George Feldman

Dedicated to kids who know that "A" for "apple" is boring; and to George's mom Ann, a reading teacher, who wanted a book like this for 50 years.

Special thanks to our talented comedic models: Theo, Ann, Yaretzi, Sophia, Deacon, Kim, Broc, Melanie, Max, Adela Lily, Reid, Nate, Molly, Deven, Elana, Ricky, Veronica, Britten, Parker, Ali, Jack, Melissa, Mindy, Janette, Terry, Richard, Piper and Mike.

Photo credits- Krishna, George & Theo Feldman, Amy, Celeste, Marilyn and Jenny.

Additional thank yous to Conchita's Ice Cream, Ohlone Otters, Watsonville Yoga, Mizunoslove, Candelaria, Maria, Alfredo, Rori and Nick.

ISBN-13: 9798361212699

Adorable animals attack starts with A.

Booger starts with B.

Cookies and candy start with C.

Dragon starts with D.

Electricity starts with E.

f

Firefighter's fart starts with F.

Gorilla's gum starts with G.

g

Hide starts with H.

Ice cream starts with I.

Jump starts with J.

Kick starts with K.

Legos® start with L.

Muddy mutt starts with M.
m

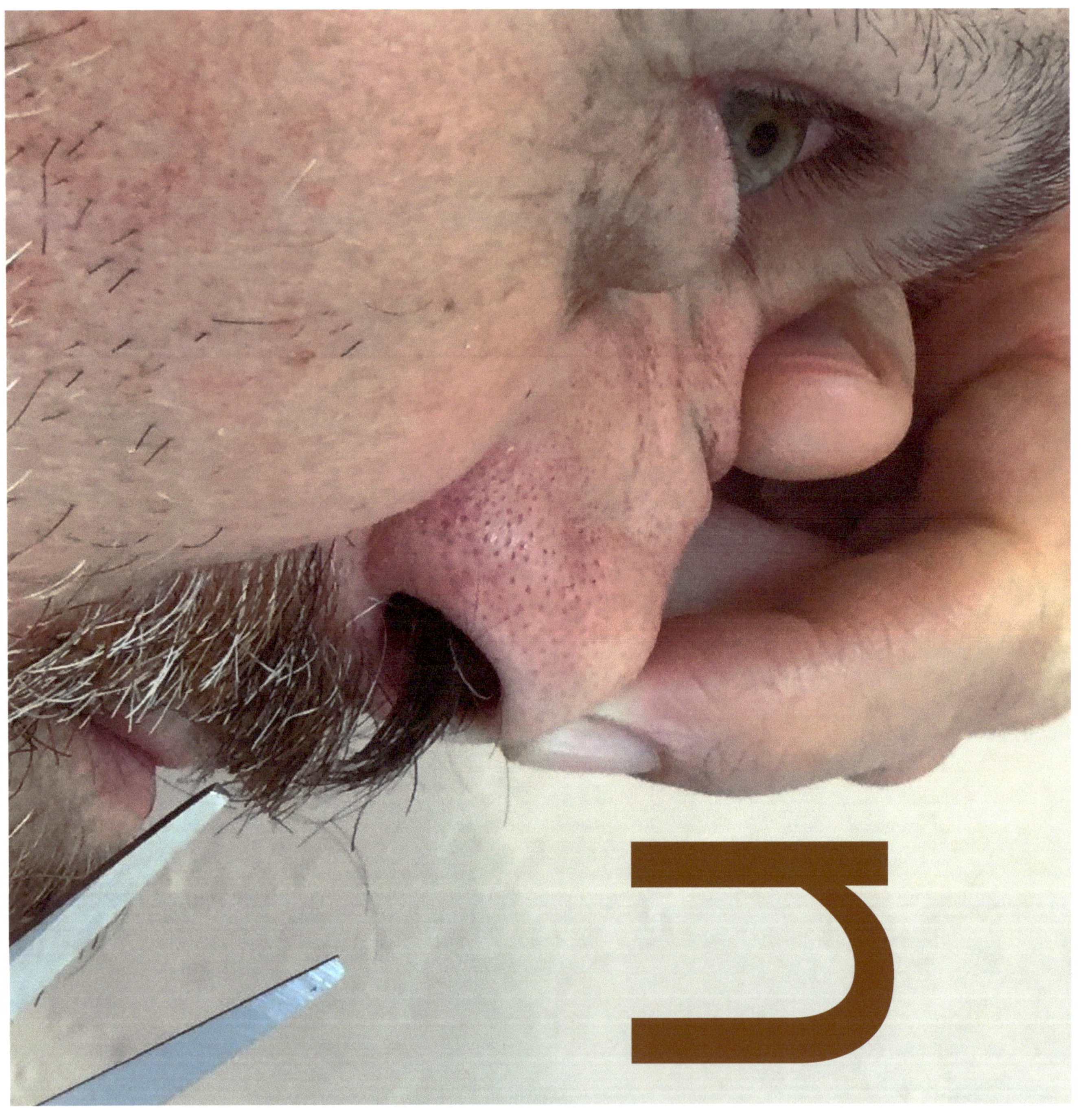
Nose hair starts with N.

Oh no and ouchies start with O.

Puppy pizza party starts with P.

Queen of quarters starts with Q.

Rainbow racers start with R.

Stinky, sandy socks start with S.

Taco truck starts with T.

Unicorns in underwear start with U.

Vomit starts with V.

WiFi starts with W.

X marks the spot starts with X.

Yuck and yum start with Y.

Zooming zebras and Zzzs start with Z.

Our other books include:

"I am Proud of My Family" (in English, Spanish, and Mixteco),

"What Do You Want To Be?" (also in English, Spanish, and Mixteco),

and the game "Auto-Destruct-O-Rama" (just in English).

You can buy all our books at Amazon.com or at Kelly's Books in Watsonville, CA.

(No puppies were given pizza during the making of this book, but one got a bath.)